Mike Walle

The Full Works

INTRODUCTION

Born in 1944, I am a resident of a small village just south of Stratford-upon-Avon, a town not lacking in literary fame. I live with my wife, Sue, to whom this book is dedicated as are a couple of the love poems it contains. Our current cherished companion is Otto, a dachshund. We have two married children and five grandchildren in whom we take inordinate pride. My education culminated in a bachelor's degree in political science, a master's degree in management and a post-graduate diploma in psychology. My professional career was in what was at that time known as personnel management. I first worked in private sector companies and then the Central Electricity Generating Board at their London headquarters. When I joined it, the CECB was State owned.

Privatisation gave me a once in a lifetime opportunity for early retirement and the chance to focus on my two primary intellectual interests: creative writing and evolution's role in determining what is known as the human condition. This book is one result of that opportunity. However, it has only come into being because of the tireless efforts of two outstanding supporters: my niece Alison Gowers who brought order out of chaos, and my friend of sixty years, Les Gallop, who showed remarkable expertise in dealing with the technicalities of self-publishing.

The linkage between poetry and evolutionary theory may not seem obvious. The common ground is human nature. I have published academic works on the way in which I believe natural selection has (a) shaped human consciousness and (b) saddled us with very negative conditions such as severe depression*. As a result of the interplay in my mind between these seemingly disparate interests, most poems in this book, from light to deadly serious, reflect aspects of our evolved natures and, in some instances, directly reflect modern evolutionary theory.

I have had a lifelong love of English literature and in turning to poetry in my fifties, I was strongly drawn to metrical forms rather than free verse. This is partly because I enjoy the challenge of meeting the very different requirements of metre and meaning at the same time. I also believe that doing so increases the effect because the two strands are picked up in different areas of the brain.

I very much hope that at least some of what I have written stimulates your interest.

Mike Waller, Preston on Stour, July 2024

* M.J.C. Waller (1996) Organisation theory and the origins of consciousness. *Journal of Social and Evolutionary Systems*, 19(10): 17-30.

M.J.C. Waller (2010) Family stigma, sexual selection and the evolutionary origins of severe depression's physiological consequences. *Journal of Social, Evolutionary, and Cultural Psychology.* 4(2): 94-114.

PART ONE

Comedy

Somethings borrowed, somethings new,
Somethings old, somethings blue

A SECOND CHANCE

I'd been twelve months retired and whilst waiting for my tea
I opened up a little pot I'd found beneath a tree.
And there, within an instant, before my tired old eyes,
Appeared a little fairy, who, to my very great surprise,
Told me she could grant a wish, but made it very plain,
The only choice available was to start my life again.
If I would trade my tired old frame, I'd get within its place,
Not just a youthful body, but a youthful mind and face.
I could find a new life's partner, build a new career
And savour all the joys of love which young folk hold so dear.

Then I thought of how I'd struggled in an easier time,
The lucky breaks I'd enjoyed, and the hills I didn't climb.
I thought about my children, my wife, my dog, my cat;
I reflected on my pension, 'cos there's naught as safe as that.
I thought about my garden, the trees, the shrubs, the pond.
Then I told that little fairy where to stick her little wand.

COUP DE GRACE

Fourteen of us were dining and I came on rather strong
Trying to correct some old coot so plainly in the wrong.
I came from every quarter to try to put him straight,
But firmly he held his ground & steadfast cleared his plate.

Although I'd hoped to win him round, it soon began to look
As if the settling of this question required a reference book.
So I took down the Britannica, but when I found the page
I saw my views were so much tosh and his were very sage.

Speechless, I did little then but to splutter and to choke,
And in no way did my suffering cease when at last, he spoke.
His comment surely placed me in the tribe that David smote:
"D'you know, before you checked it, I knew that's what I wrote".

THE SPIRIT OF COMPROMISE

She was a girl of firm resolve, who knew her right from wrong;
Confronted by temptation, she was resolute and strong.
She set herself a golden rule, as befits a girl of rank:
He to whom she gave her hand needs thousands in the bank.
On this she pressed her latest beau and told him not to bluff;
But when she heard "Just fifteen quid" she thought it close
enough!

A PROPER TYKE

A true born son of Yorkshire went amidst those foreign hordes
To visit that famous holy place that some folk still call "Lords".
He arrived in a wheelchair, but soon filled the town with talk
By rising from its metal frame to very nimbly walk.
But his son, one Sidney Barnsthwaite, then had to ask his dad
Why, instead of being joyous, he looked so very sad?
"Thy'll never be a proper Tyke" the old man growled at Sid,
"I've not long had yon wheelchair and it cost me forty quid".

A MISCONCEPTION

Father says to daughter she ought to understand
That Dolly comes with boyfriend Ben, not with Sergeant Bland
Daughter said to father, whilst playing with her toy,
"Dolly fake's it with the boyfriend but comes with soldier boy!"

JUST DESSERTS

(With acknowledgements to Stanley Baxter)

He told her of his secret dream
To coat her, naked, in thick cream.
How first he'd make a spongy bed
All soaked in syrup, base to head,
And then - oh the evil bustard -
He'd lay 'er in fruit and custard.
She recumbent, he'd make merry
Splashing out on nuts and sherry.
But such talk was much in error;
Soon he stood there, white with terror.
For she proved, by use of rifle,
Not a girl with whom to trifle.

A SOLAR PARADOX

Written when the EU embargoed British meat products embargoed because of 'mad cow disease'.

I am THE British tabloid. I always tell the truth.
A pox on all the broadsheets, so prissy and aloof.
I stand for British interests and naked female flesh;
I thrive on sex 'n violence and not much Bangladesh.
If European partners strike our trade a blow,
From my printing house in Wapping I'll soon let them know
They must eat up all our beefsteak*, every truck and boat,
And if they starts to cavil, I'll 'ave 'em by the throat.
But if those same old foreigners sends us rotten stuff,
I'll thump 'em and I'll bash 'em until they've 'ad enough.
It matters not what kind of stuff, you know the line I'll take:
"There'll be no foreign profits if British health's at stake!"
In this you see a paradox? 'Tis very soon resolved,
When Mr Murdoch 'phones me, I do just what I'm told.

ADULTERATED LOVE

I love thee my little whippet,
Thou art the fairest thing I've seen.
Yet when thy tongue doth brush my lips
I can't help thinking where it's been!

AN ACT OF GALLANTRY

A rich man's only son met a sad friend of his sister.
When she offered up her lips, he took the chance and kissed her.
His act was kind and not debauched, as I feared you might suppose,
'Cos he had to plant his kiss near two dewdrops on her nose.

PRE-DECIMAL LIAISONS

The late Miss Tallulah Bankhead, star of stage & screen,
Had a very ready wit, although 'twas a shade obscene.
A very famous beauty, she was absolutely sure
That no man born could resist her great allure.
Some pals, the little vixens, deciding to doubt her word,
Named one whose inclinations made her claim absurd.
But Tallulah was a fighter and gave her solemn bond
She'd stake a level pound that she could raise his wand.

The sordid tryst is over and Miss Bankhead's in a fix;
But given what she has achieved, she asks for 12/6d*.

62.5p

BILLS

The trouble with accountancy
Is fate's intention I should see
Each month some nasty little debt
I haven't even thought of yet.

The telly's down, my specs are weak,
My "Y" fronts sag towards my feet;
A tyre's bald, a window's blown,
My cash is to the four winds sown.

The statement's come, the pension's in,
I should be living like a king!
But there too, lying by the door,
The buff clad fiends which make me poor.

SOLVING THE PROBLEM

The fire in our Cropthorne home never did draw true.
Regardless of the fuel we used, or how we cleaned the flue,
It blacked us up like miners and filled the place with soot;
So I fetched a firm from Worcester to come and have a look.

They fitted on a gadget which they said would make it clean,
But, as next time we lit it, it seemed they had never been,
They had to send another chap who mainly seemed to curse
'Cos though he did his level best, he only made it worse.

When I saw old Arthur who had kept our pub for years,
And told him that this dratted fire brought my wife to tears.
He said it weren't the fire's fault, it were the blooming wind
It swoops & swirls around us just like the Shropshire Mynd.

He said, though not a cure, a big difference could be made
By any man who's handy with a barrow, pick and spade.
First, I stared in some confusion, then with looks to kill,
'Cos what he told me, laughing, was to dig up Bredon Hill!

BRICKS

When I was small, all bricks were toys
That parents mainly gave to boys
To show them how a house is made
If course on course is caref'ly laid.

At school I thought a "brick" a friend
Whose staunch support would never end;
But even though I'd search and search,
Mine mostly left me in the lurch.

When wed, bricks, combined with mortar,
Are seen as things we really ought'a
Pile in all the cash we can
Then pay the rest by mortgage plan.

Now, at eighty, all alone,
Bereft of wife, shorn of home,
What I need are bricks of gold
To pay the fees they charge the old!

DAS KAPITAL

His ragged shirt, his ragged shorts could not keep out the cold;
Yet he burned with an inner fire from all that he'd been told.
'Tween grimy setts and leaden sky, he'd seen a thing sublime:
An orator who boldly said that property's a crime.

And when the speaker ceased the young boy straightway went
To ask for more examples of what socialism meant.
The speaker used "house" & "car" as cases where he reckoned
That if by chance he had two, he'd give the boy the second.

His listener found these instances a bit too far removed,
So asked about domestic pigs - a source of cash and food.
Ashen, the orator tersely spoke then pushed off towards his digs,
"Push off you little varmint, I've got two bloody pigs".

CHAIR DODGER

He was what we called a clippie, but on a Yankee bus;
For twenty years he took the fares with very little fuss.
But then one night a drunkard went a bit too far
So he pushed him from the platform, beneath a speeding car.
His defence was very shaky and, although the trial was fair,
He knew before they told him, he'd be sentenced to the chair.
As they prepared him for old smoky, he ate his last request,
A large hand of ripe bananas, the fruit which he liked best.
But when they threw the switch on, he didn't get a jolt
Although they tried it two more times, they couldn't raise a volt.
This meant that they must free him, but really had to know
What had been the clever trick which made the chair not go.
Was it the bananas which upset their famed destructor?
"No" he said "Twas bound to fail; I'm such a bad conductor!".

CHOSEN WITH MALICIOUS CARE

For my little niece Matilda I have found the very thing,
A pretty little picture of a kitten chasing string.
There's no harm in now reminding her she used to have a cat
Until that petrol tanker squashed it flatter than a mat.

Then there is Quentin Biggleswade who always yearned to fly,
Turned down by the RAF when they found his lazy eye.
The book that I chose for him, I picked with special care,
It's from the Reader's Digest and called "Heroes of the Air".

Poor Paul, who got the numbers right but lost the little slip,
Obsessed by all the cash he's missed, is quickly losing grip.
For him I've found a video showing life isn't such a bitch.
By the nice folk at "Hello", it's called "Lifestyles of the Rich".

Finally, there is Cousin Jean, who wed that chap from Arles;
A bandy little Frenchman with crooked teeth and piles.
The 12 months she spent with him were cruelty unrefined.
One way she's found of coping is to wipe it from her mind.
The present I've just sought out for her simply cannot fail;
'A Year in Provence', that book by Peter Mayle.

COUNTRY MAGIC

I was spinning down to Brighton for a quiet weekend's fling,
When some kind of long-eared creature collided with my wing.
I could have hit the pedal hard and left the thing for dead,
But I knew for sure it would not do just to press ahead.
Instead I turned and there I found a man in country clothes,
Kneeling beside the wounded beast in what seemed its final throes.

Yet when he drenched it in a liquid from an ancient silver flask
It revived within an instant, so straightway I had to ask:
"Though if its a precious secret, you clearly must refuse,
I'd love to know what's in the balm that I've just seen you use".
"Why bless zee sir, to tell you this won't leave me any poorer,
Oi buys it at the Chemist, them calls it hare restorer".

DESCENT OF MAN

Imagine an ancient robber who preyed upon the dead
And found within the Vale of Kings a golden pharaoh's head.
He had no home, he had no school, he could not read or write,
Yet even he wept softly as he worked by tallow light.
As it sunk within his smelter, he slunk from where he'd stood
Because he had turned to bullion a thing that looked so good.
Imagine now a future thief in what was London Town
Who digs & delves for treasure where the Tate has tumbled down.
Like a crow in search of pickings, he sees what luck will bring;
But in twenty days of effort he only finds one thing.
The Egyptian saw great beauty, but he would feel accursed
Were that one piece of carrion a sheep by Damien Hirst.

DIABOLICAL CONFUSION

See two nuns, whose car is burnished bright,
Hastening home before the fall of night.
Then, astride the bonnet, appears the dreadful fiend,
His loathsome form besmirching all they'd cleaned.
Fork, wings, pointed tail, eyes to make you freeze;
Stench not sulf'rous, but more like rancid cheese.
The elder sister, never at a loss,
Says very calmly, "Show the brute your cross".
Puzzled, then shocked at what she thought this meant,
Her companion wound down the window, leant
Out, and said in a voice which carried far,
"Oi, you, Devil, get off our bloody car!"

DOORS

I love the doors of cheap cafes and places they brew hops,
As well as doors of super stores and those of bakers' shops.
I love the doors of swish hotels and little country inns,
And also doors of shady joints that hide all kinds of sins.

As well as doors on foreign shores, I love all those of home,
Including that most famous door named as Durdle's own.
But, save for the doors of paradise, should I have such luck,
The fairest Dors I'll ever see was Miss Diana Fluck.*

The birth name of the blond bombshell, Diana Dors.

THE NEW HELEN

The face that launched a thousand ships
and burned a thousand towers,
Now watches Coronation Street and wastes a thousand hours.
I think that she should gird herself, step outside the door,
Captivate some foreign guy and start another war.

ELEMENTARY, DEAR WATSON

The famous Doctor Watson and his pal from Baker Street
Were camping down in Surrey as a kind of Easter treat.
Waking from their slumbers they saw through bleary eyes
A hundred thousand twinkling stars spread across the skies.

When Sherlock asked the Doctor: "What does this all mean?"
It was the kind of question he yearned for in his dreams.
For though his brain responded slowly, of facts it was a mine
So he thought showing this would be his chance to shine.

He first declared the stars told him that we are not alone
Every planet they sustained could not be lifeless stone.
He next spoke on star-signs and their claimed effects on life
Saying that he doubted this but it much impressed his wife.

He turned to navigation, saying stars helped those at sea
And he'd just deduced from them that it was half past three.
Then he touched on meteorology and said a clear night sky
Would make it almost certain next day'd be bright and dry.

Finally, he spoke of God whose tireless strength and love
Had fashioned all the firmament they saw so clear above.
"You dozy fool" said Sherlock, his patience now all spent,
'Cos what they saw revealed to him a thief had nicked their tent!

MISSION IMPOSSIBLE

After several days of searching for a little dog who'd strayed,
I found it dead within a trap some evil fiend had laid.
So I chose to use my father's ring, his dying gift to me,
Which, when a secret phrase is said, can set a genie free.
Told of the problem, he said he could not raise up the dead,
But he'd now been summoned, he'd grant another wish instead.
Now, as readers will attest, I'm a poet of great skill,
Yet, enormous though my talent is, the laurels lie with Will.
So I said to the genie: "I'll not ask for very much;
Just give me the extra skills to match old Shakespeare's touch".
Strangely, rather than attempt a task like falling off a log,
The genie, turning on his heels, said: "Let's recheck the dog".

FALSE EXPECTATIONS

Rosie was a wicked girl who had got three teachers sacked
By pulling clever little scams and twisting all the facts.
And now she had the Science man so firmly in her sights
That, sensing easy victory, she'd almost wet her tights.

He'd asked which was the organ that swelled ten times in size
Depending on the stimulus which passed before the eyes.
She saw this as a golden chance and said she'd tell the Head
And, once branded as a pervert, he might as well be dead.

But he just turned and asked the same of little Ellie May
Whose shining face of innocence had often made his day.
"The answer, Sir's, the iris which, depending on the light,
Can broaden out to pencil-wide or close up needle-tight."

He then turned back to Rosie whose face was ashen grey
And nor was she much comforted by what he had to say:
"Two things I must tell you: First, you're both crude & cruel.
Second, if that's what you're expecting, you'll get no joy at all".

WHAT DR WHO OUGHT TO DO

Each time I see the fragment that's Pershore Abbey Church
I think I should embark upon a very thorough search
For all the laws pertaining to that wonderful machine
That battles with the tides of time 'til bygone days are seen.
I would not search out secrets, golden plate or coin,
I'd simply find King Harry's place and knee him in the groin.

IT ALL VANISHED – JUST LIKE THAT!

(With acknowledgements to the late Tommy Cooper).

A Stradivarius and Rubens had just been left to me,
And I thought that if I sold them I should at last be free.
No longer tightly tied within the weary world of toil;
No longer cruelly forced, encaged, to pace my native soil.
I seemed to sense the southern seas, the rustling of the palms,
And, deep within my reverie, those soft, compliant arms.
So later, when I learned the truth, it left me more than sad:
Rubens made the violin; it's the painting that's a Strad!

HOLE-IN-ONE

Two white-bearded patriarchs and a thirty-something man
Were hacking round the golf course short on skill and plan.
The first so miss-struck his ball it was nowhere to be seen,
Until a raven seized the thing and dropped it on the green.

The young man's found the lake, but not sinking like a brick,
It sat resting on the surface whilst he performed the trick
Of walking on the water just as if it were a floor
And, still standing on the lake top, he drove it to the shore.

But the third contender's hole-in-one put these in the shade.
His careless action off the tee implied he'd never played;
But as the little golf-ball commenced it aimless flight,
Any casual passer-by would have seen a wondrous sight.

The earth reshaped itself, so when it tumbled from the air
It found the hole, the pin and green all snugly lying there.
Then Moses said to Jesus "I know saying this is bad,
But it is a little pointless, us playing with your Dad.

KITCHEN NONSENSE

Oh what should we do with the kettle?
A kettle's a wonderful beast.
I think we should boil it in oil
And then have a marvellous feast.

Oh what should we do with the oven?
An oven's a glorious chum.
I think we should coat it in butter
And leave it to fry in the sun.

Oh what should we do with the washer?
It makes such marvellous toast.
I think we should fill it with mustard
And take a quick spin to the coast.

Oh what should we do with the table?
It has such wonderful legs.
I think we should tempt it with mackerel
To see if it sits up and begs.

Oh what should we do with the kitchen?
It will go round and around.
I think that we'll take it to market
And sell it for twenty-three pound.

LINGUISTIC ERROR

A little Miss from Camden Town, convinced we'd lose the war,
Thought siding with the German's a wiser course for sure.
Instead of finding war work, and trying to do her bit,
She sought, seduced, then married a little man called Smit.

Least it was what she thought she'd done, the over-hasty fool.
Then she read his papers and found he wasn't "Smit" at all.
Born a "Smith" in Bethnal Green, her little cockney poppet,
Everywhere an "H" appeared, he couldn't help but drop it.

IT'S NOT WHAT I SAY …..

Oh how I hate the modern world
Which, ever since its flag unfurled,
Has showered us with tasteless tat
And fed the poor on processed fat.

Oh how I loath our modern lives
Where every worker strives and strives
Acquiring things they do not need,
An appetite we're taught to feed.

So when resting in my country home
I often find my thoughts will roam
To selling up my New York loft
And heading North to buy a croft.

But then I see it isn't right
So lamely to give up the fight.
There's many mountains still to climb;
So many things to stamp as mine!

OUT OF THE MOUTH OF BABES

Imagine a little boy of four who knelt beside his bed
As father stood outside the door to hear the prayers he said.
The child gave a simple list of those the Lord should save,
But then he spoke as if his aunt lay cold within her grave.

As father thought the aunt was well, he got nasty shock
When, next morn, she passed away, at just on five o'clock.
Again at prayer, Gramps is dead, the child seems to think;
And although Dad, who overhears, is sure he is in the pink.

But, next day, at bang on five, the old man met his maker,
And, once more outside the door, Dad hears a bigger shaker.
"May my father rest in peace" was what the youngster said,
Which left the father certain sure that he'd, by dawn, be dead.

Though he died a myriad deaths as the clock crept up to five,
That hour had come, and slowly gone, and he was still alive.
At eight o'clock he left for work, sure he'd out-foxed his fate;
It was then he saw the milkman slumped dead across the gate.

THE TRUE STORY OF A MIRACLE CURE

My grandma, who was past her peak,
Saw Dr Smith three times a week.
The medic never let her down
And for each call charged half-a-crown.
Then suddenly, Oh God be praised,
He came but once in fourteen days.
Was grandma's case a famous cure,
Or were his thoughts a bit less pure?
'Cos at just the time that he called less
Old Bevan launched the NHS.

ONE IN A MILLION

"I know that I am special; I know than I'm unique.
I know that I'll condemn my friends to envy laced with pique.
I know that when they see me, folks will say I'm mad;
By which is meant my life is rich whilst theirs is dull and sad.

I know that had they seen me, my parents would be proud
As I, the finest of their sons, stand nobly from the crowd."
'Twas then he heard the old cook say, "Come on my little man,
Pop out from your cosy pod and drop straight in the pan".

'ORRIBLE TRAGEDY AT BLACKPOOL

I speak of a town called Blackpool, that's famous for glitter and tat,
Where chips are a staple of diet and trippers have words on their hat.
I speak of a family named Grendall who took young Alan to see
A place they consider as sacred as St Paul's and the Abbey's to me.
To avoid a shower they entered the Tower and
sought out everything free.
When they started to tire no chairs would they hire
but sat on some stones by the sea.
It was then that a wave took that boy oh so brave
and swept him out with the tide.
With this event so traumatic it seemed automatic
that Ma just sat there and cried.
But don't mistakenly think to see the boy sink
caused her poor heart to crack.
For 'tis my belief what caused her the grief
was the wave that washed him back.

THE ANSWER IS DRAWLING IN THE WIND

Headline: King Penguins beat scientists to it - applied maths used to counter wind "noise".

The penguin was a sorry bird
Whose calls of love could not be heard
Above those savage polar gales
Of which we've read in traveller's tales.
Such birds must part to do their tasks,
But when their cries the cruel wind masks
They soon cease searching for their mate,
Become depressed and vegetate.

Now even in our temp'rate climes
A single mum has quite hard times;
So think of those in polar wastes
Whose young depend on fish-based pastes.
They cannot fish and warm their brood,
So chicks succumb for want of food;
A parlous state, says one old scribe,
That threatened all the penguin tribe.

The answer for those hapless mums
Was found by penguins doing sums.
They noted that a hurricane
Will drop in tempo, now'n again
So whilst still screeching like the gulls,
They draw it out in search of lulls.
They lengthen not by rule of thumb,
But work precisely, sum by sum.

As up each mile the windspeed goes
Their cries' attenuation grows.
In short, they have the kind of skill
With which we humans struggle still.
There is but one thing I can't see,
- Perhaps you'll make it clear to me.
If with maths they're more than rookies
Why aren't penguins down the bookies?

POETIC LICENCE

Why waste a day in searching for one word?
Why face the insolence of naked page?
Why seek to please the all too fickle herd?
Why struggle with both impotence and rage?

So I didn't.

THERE'S ONLY ONE ANSWER

Once I touched a poet's skull; I did it just to see
Whether that which made her great would flow from it to me.
Then I sought out a poet's bust, a carved and polished stone,
To see if I could steal his muse and make the thing my own.

Next I searched a poet's bed, my reasoning's clear, of course.
I hoped within its many springs to find the poet's source.
Lastly - to my undying shame - I stole a poet's quill.
I thought, perhaps, some golden words might lie within it still.

But much too late I came to see this all a waste of time.
You cannot capture by such means thoughts of one sublime.
Bones, busts, beds and quills don't warrant second looks;
To find what makes some poets great, just read their bloody books.

NOT QUITE WHAT HE INTENDED

A pious country preacher-man was striding down the trail,
Rock-solid in the sure belief his Lord would never fail.
Then suddenly, up ahead he saw some fearsome grizzly bears,
Who fixed upon the preacher cruel and hungry stares.

Unable to out-pace the brutes, the man implored his Lord
To introduce religious thoughts within that bearish horde.
Lo, the bears began to pray, crouched down on all four feet:
"We praise thee, Lord, we praise thee, Lord,
for what we're about to eat".

ONE TO AMUSE THE VICAR

It was wedding day in heaven; t'would be a wondrous sight.
All the loves which should have been,
would be joined in God that night.
But before it even started, they had to stop the feast;
Though any kind would suit them, they could not find a priest.

THE RIGHT PRIORITIES

I stumbled from the Court of Law, a sad and broken man.
She'd got the house, the car, the cash & half my pension plan.
I slunk into my local to drown out the fairer sex,
But there I found, awaiting me, my second cousin's ex-.

She said when she heard my news she'd cried 'n cried 'n cried.
If she'd found a man like me, she'd have kept him 'til she died.
And though she thought my wife a friend, she really had to say
Her kind of greedy selfishness had surely had its day.

In life she'd learnt girls should give & never count the cost;
To measure love in days well spent and not careers they'd lost.
Her kindly words, the whisky mac, revitalised my heart;
I wondered why, in times gone by, I took my cousin's part.

I touched her knee, I raised my glass and said with little fuss:
"Here's to the months and years ahead, and you and I as us".
With shining eyes & husky voice she spoke as glasses chinked:
"My love, that part-pension you've got left, is it index-linked?"

ROUND OBJECTS

or
Who's going to tell him?

A young heaven-born from Oxford, his feet on blotter pad,
Sat using half his intellect and feeling rather glad
That he'd joined the Foreign Office and not some dreary beat
Concerned with coal, cabbages, or the health of children's feet.

Whilst savouring his good fortune, he felt so well deserved,
On the page which lay before him he suddenly observed
An error of reasoning so spectacularly wrong
That his note within the margin was somewhat over strong.

But at least he wrote "Round objects" and not that little word
So loved by bolshie thinkers and the very common herd.

In sixteen weeks, via sixteen hands, that self-same paper rose
Until at the highest level his comment came to pose
A thorny little problem 'cos, a man of sober mien,
The Secretary of State thought that swearing was unclean.

And having seen the fateful words, he wrote to this effect:
"Pray tell me, who is this Round and why does he object?"

THE BEE HAS QUIT THE CLOVER

The worker bees have gone on strike, so all the keepers shout.
We ask them why those little chaps downed tools & flew off out.
The keepers say that though we laugh, it really isn't funny.
What they want is shorter flowers and a big increase in honey.

TWO ROWS IN FRONT

Two lovers sitting side by side
With urgent passins they don't hide.
A touch, a squeeze, a ling'ring kiss,
Then whispered words confirming bliss.
"A pretty sight" there's some who'd say;
But I'd prefer they watched the play!

CEREAL KILLER

She said before she left him, "I'll give you one last tip,
Because you are the kind of fella' most girls give the slip.
If you want to try again, apply this simple trick,
Pick yourself a widow, as they're the kind who stick.
So he wed a second time, but bliss did not last long
As she spiked his bowl of porridge with poison rather strong.

So if you'd wed a widow, yet wish to stay alive,
Avoid a girl of twenty-three to whom you're number five.

AN UNFORTUNATE SLIP

He said with cheery confidence "Our postman's having fun,
They say he's scored in every house except, of course, for one".
His wife, somewhat distracted, spoke whilst pouring out the tea,
"Oh, that'll be the snotty cat who lives at forty-three".

A STUDIED RESPONSE

Two fearful souls, just freed from Earth, stand by Heaven's gate.
With trembling hands & downcast eyes, each awaits his fate.
But Peter's got a problem, his scanner's on the blink
Whilst knowing what each did, he can't tell what they think.
Though Heaven hates a broken reed and doesn't let them in,
St. Peter felt a long delay would be a greater sin.
So he guarantees their entry, but at a later date,
Because first, he'll fix the scanner whilst they go back and wait,
As he must have the details that are needed to ensure
That everything goes smoothly when they enter Heaven's door.

By way of compensation, he then granted them the boon
As to what they became whilst waiting, each could call the tune.
Whilst the first chose an eagle, his companion chewed the cud,
Then, with slow deliberation, said he thought he'd be a stud.
St. Peter, although suffused with rage, didn't raise a storm
And each, within an instant, took up his chosen form.
Now, there you see the eagle above that mountain crest
Where the wonders of creation swell out his feathered breast.
But the fate of his companion is in a different class;
See him? In the snow tyre of that car that climbs the pass!

SUGAR

"Sugar", the old man said, "be it in coffee, be it in bed,
So lacks subtlety that it can only turn a young man's head.
We wise old birds, our taste buds much the more mature,
Seek out the savour of experience, not the pure,
Cloying, naiveté of shallow, untested youth".
And having spoken, he smiled, as does one imparting truth.

But listener, here is a footnote that I am bound to share:
It must be said that soon he fled with a pretty, Swiss au pair.

LATERAL THINKING

A golden-headed eight year old was playing in the soil
Whilst grandpa, in his deck chair, observed his earnest toil.
The boy espied a garden worm just poking out its head
And having gently pulled it free as though it were a thread,
He turned toward his grandpa expecting lavish praise,
But instead the old man told him, he must, if aiming to amaze,
Return the little creature to the hole from whence it came,
Using some kindly means that would neither kill nor maim.

He sought by this to teach a truth, but being very bright,
The boy fetched a hair spray can, stretched the worm out tight,
Sprayed on several coatings; and, as soon as these had dried,
He slid the worm into the hole and left it snug inside.
Two things surprised the boy. First, grandpa looked so canny.
And, next day beside his breakfast egg,
was ten quid from his granny.

THE STAR-GAZER'S LAMENT

(With acknowledgements to the late Les Dawson)

I sat besides my Uncle Wilf as he breathed out his last,
And sensing that it was the end, he railed against the past.
Between savage self-reproaches and cruelly anguished cries,
I learned that his besetting sin was gazing at the skies.

Whilst others schemed and studied to keep the wolf at bay,
He had scattered all his chances down the Milky Way.
Though Venus led his schoolmates to mortgage, kids and car,
To my dear departing uncle, it remained the Morning Star.
And now he'd come to realise it had been a wasted life,
He had to face the great abyss sans honours, child or wife.

Yet the poignancy of his parting had a nobler side;
As, raised up upon his pillow, he very bravely tried
To give me certain guidance, with what proved his final breath,
To guard against the uselessness which stigmatised his death:
"Be guided, boy, be guided by this glistening pearl of truth,
If you build an outside toilet, make sure it's got a roof!

STAND BY YOUR MAN

My pride and joy's a whippet, a girl of sinewed grace,
Who's small enough when cradled to caress against my face.
At rest, she seems imperious, an animated sphinx;
Unleashed, she's like an arrow, or a kind of canine lynx.

Upon seeing my devotion, my wife demands to know
Would it now matter much were she to up and go.
But I quickly make it clear to her it simply isn't done
To walk out on your husband when his whippet needs a mum.

THERE'S MORE THAN ONE WAY.......

A care-worn little grandma, somewhat tired and grey
Came to see her Doctor on a bright, clear, springtime day,
And said that she had a need for pills ladies call in aid
To ensure that in their love-life, no little bairns are made.
Her answer when he asked her "Why?" seemed clearly less than true.
"To cure my insomnia." she declared, that's something they don't do.
But then she went on to say: "My grandchild's a teenage girl
Whose very active social life has become an endless whirl.
And now she has a boyfriend, a very randy dog,
So, a tablet in her porridge and I'll be sleeping like a log!"

TIMES CHANGE: A PRECAUTIONARY TALE

Headline: Female Violence Increasing

The late Mr Jeffrey Bernard, the life of whom was low,
Once wrote about a publican who, many years ago,
Pulled, within that sacred place some ladies call their lavvie
A scam which though despicable, was very strong on savvy.
He mounted on an inside wall a machine of painted tin
And though it said it held supplies, he never put them in.
This cost the women very dear and no doubt made then cross;
But, as the wicked landlord knew, they'd not reclaim their loss
'Cos in those days a lady would lose all her social clout
Once shown to be complying with the motto of the scout.

But know ye modern shysters who'd thus bilk the fairer sex,
The little flowers we've raised up would break your bloody necks!

THURBER'S UNICORN ELABORATED

A poetic rendering of a story originally told by James Thurber.

He crept out from his marriage bed, a place of grief and shame,
To gaze upon the only thing that soothed his endless pain.
He looked upon his garden where each week he toiled for hours
To draw on the secret strength derived from plants and flowers.
And there, grazing by his rose bed, he saw the fairest sight:
A proud and stately unicorn whose coat was purest white.

He was witnessing great beauty, so wished to share his joy
As what he'd seen was flesh 'n blood, and not some tawdry toy.
But his wife, on being told of this, stayed laying in her bed,
Claiming seeing unicorns just meant strangeness in the head.
She said this proved him a booby, one she would soon dispatch
To join all the other boobies inside the booby-hatch.

She then called the doctor and those with coats of white
Who carry with them straps & bonds in case their patients fight.
She told them of the "unicorn" which he had said he'd seen.
But when they spoke to him of this, he struck a puzzled mien;
And though she assailed him with the cruellest of cruel looks,
He said: "Surely that's the kind of beast only found in books?".

At this his wife exploded and so beat him round the head
That, trussed up like a chicken, she was carted off instead.
From this Thurber drew a moral which I'll not seek to match:
"Never count your boobies until they're safely in the hatch"

THEY SAID THE DUTCH.........

They said the Dutch were out of touch when they took on the sea,
But those smart tykes soon built the dykes & got their farmland free.
They said the Swiss were most remiss in confronting Gestler's crowd,
But under Tell, they fought like hell, so now they're free and proud.
They said those Scots must all be pots to challenge Edward One,
But once King Bruce was on the loose, those English had to run.
So if your Auntie Molly says off your trolley you have surely come,
Get on your feet and say tout sweet that she is clearly dumb.

OLD TOM'S TALE

When I was in my savage prime, I held the world in thrall;
But now I'm old and broken and there's no respect at all.
I've heard that violence doesn't pay and lots of stuff like that;
But I say it damned well does - especially for a cat!

THEORY AND PRACTICE

He was a very naughty boy and up to every trick.
He wasn't curbed by kindly words or liberal use of stick.
But what made his poor old father routinely hit the roof
Was his seeming inability to ever tell the truth.

Then, as in a blinding flash, an answer struck the dad.
Might examples drawn from history change his wayward lad?
He spoke to him of Washington, who escaped entirely free
And all because he told the truth about that cherry tree.

Now, a river flowed by their home and on its banks there stood
An ancient outside toilet that was largely made of wood.
To this the boy attached a line which he'd very tightly tied
To the towing-hitch of a great big truck parked the other side.

He didn't see what happened as he had to go to school,
But when his father questioned him, he did not lie at all.
But sadly, though doing this had now seemed the smarter card,
An angry, red-faced parent then hit him rather hard.

His father had an answer when asked why he struck the blow
Instead of doing as did George's dad all those years ago.
"Can't you see the difference, my foolish little clown?
His pa weren't up the tree when the blighter chopped it down!"

THE WICKED SQUIRE

There was once a squire called Pretty
A seducer who worked without pity.
Nor did he stop
At one village crop,
He de-flowered three towns and a city.

MAN OF DESTINY

There once was as archer named Hugh
Whose shots very rarely flew true.
Though on Harold's side,
His arrow went wide,
And changed the whole course of British history.

AURAL SEX

A chap somewhat shy and reserved
Had a wife who was quite well preserved.
Told "Remember you're forty"
She thought he said "naughty",
So he got what he hadn't deserved.

THE ITALIAN WAITER

When our foolish friend Frances agreed to a dance
The wicked headwaiter seized on the chance.
She knew in an instance it had to be wrong;
He'd lost half his teeth and he had a strange pong.
But he whirled her and swirled her, and held her up tight;
He whispered sweet nothings and his plans for the night.
As to what happened after the ball,
Frances insists that she can't recall.
But the waiter lies broken, shattered and spent.
The life force has left him and his body is bent.
And there's something of Francis we cannot ignore:
The smile on her face is as wide as a door.

STUFF THE BRIGHT SIDE

Those sports who claim that life's a game
So very rarely think the same
When they're the ones engulfed in mire,
Or theirs the house that's just caught fire.

Those clowns who say "You've got to laugh"
All seem to throw away that staff
When, on encount'ring rough terrain,
They are the ones who feel the pain.

Much the same is also true
Of idiots who say to you,
When life's all black and cash is tight,
"Just focus on the side that's bright".

Such daft remarks, all coined by fools,
Though offered up as golden rules,
Are often used by those who try
To patronise the other guy.

COLLEGE REUNION

When we were young I used to dream
That I as king and you as queen,
Both dwelling in some perfect land,
Would always journey hand in hand.

But then you found a richer lord
Whose ample coffers could afford
The very many things in life
Demanded by the perfect wife.

And now our class of '57,
Who'll next convene, I think, in Heaven,
All back within the Alma Mater,
I watch you devour your starter.

You've lost that lovely elfin face –
God knows the tonnage you displace –
And seeing what life's done to you,
I slowly mouth a silent "Phew".

But then your eyes inform my brain
That your reaction's much the same.
They seem to say I'm such a geek,
Twas you who had the narrow squeak.

Thus ex-lovers - out to grass -
Each vie to make that final pass.
The prize, no tryst beneath the moon,
But who deserves the wooden spoon.

A RABBIT'S EYE VIEW

Examination question:
State three things that a living rabbit does
that a toy rabbit cannot do?

I've been 10 weeks inside this hatch, a stinking, foetid hole,
And it's mainly been your mother who's brought my daily bowl.
Now, because it's homework, you come to ask what rabbits do
Which, if claimed for automata, would simply not be true.

First, we seek out our fuel supplies which, deep inside our tum,
Convert to forms of energy which let us breathe and run.
Second, we reproduce ourselves, indeed for that we're famed;
And, third, rabbits all have feelings, be they wild or tamed.

Compare this with a mechanism, battery powered or spring,
And you'll soon see the difference 'tween rabbits and a thing.
But I'm a truthful little chap, so must suggest to you
Some things beyond these toys are better not to do.

They can't be given the M disease, or eaten up in pies;
and nor can nasty substances be tested in their eyes.

Oh, I see that I've upset you; forget what I've just said.
Please put from mind the second three and use the first instead.

ALL TOO FAMILIAR

The morrow was the date they wed and on that special day
She'd give her man a parrot as he would often say
He thought them a special breed that had the power of speech,
A remarkable attainment that few other birds could reach.
She found one in a pet shop, the seller's price was fair,
It had come from a bawdy house, a truth he chose to share.
She thought that very funny and put it in the shed,
Then placed it in the hallway when the rest were all in bed.
Next morn it called her 'Madam' & she laughed for all her worth
And when it called her daughters 'girls' that added to the mirth.
But all the fun and jollity were very quickly gone
When on seeing her dear husband, the parrot called him 'Ron'.

HE OVER-REACHED HIMSELF

A resident of Harley Street, a doctor of renown,
Went down to check his country house, & left his wife in town.
He thought he heard a cat cry out as he passed by his well,
But reaching down to rescue it, he lost his grip and fell.
On learning he'd a broken arm, his wife said on the phone:
"In future you just heal the sick and leave the well alone".

HOPELESS CASE

To save my brain, it is my habit
To take a daily folic tablet.
But now I wonder if, Gawd Dammit,
I have already been and 'ad it.

UPDATED 'FARMER'S SONG'

The townie with cash cuts quite a dash
and is never reluctant to crow,
He lives like a swell and is destined for Hell
to burn by the fires so slow.

Of his pitiful cries as heat seers his eyes we
farmers will not want to know.
But into his pocket we go like a rocket
to pay for the stuff that we grow.

And if he gets bold and says that we've sold
the right to do as we like,
We'll holler and swear and say it ain't fair
and tell him to get on his bike.

BLUE MEANS STOP!

"Your eyes are so blue" to the charmer they said,
"How brightly they gleam when we turn your head!"
But where they saw blue they should have seen red
As they all came to learn as they climbed from his bed.

KEEP BRITAIN TIDY

I picked a little bogie and flicked it on a tree.
It landed by a spider who had it for his tea.
I am sure you've got the message, as I knew you would.
If you must throw out your rubbish, make sure it does some good!!

NOT THE ANSWER

He lent outside his window having drunk a lot of beer
And fell astride a garden fence and lost his wedding gear.
The surgeon who was hopeful said he needn't be a monk
If they could source from somewhere a baby Jumbo's trunk.
The zoo proved most helpful as they had one just die
So the surgeon took the appendage and said that he would try.
It very clearly did the job and the man went on his way
But very soon he came back and said he rued the day
He'd had the new attachment as it made his life a farce
By seeking buns at teatime to stuff them up his arse.

KISMET

Looking in her crystal ball, she said food would cause his end;
But as his girth was then so great that he could hardly bend
He did not believe she had seen through Future's tight-barred door,
But worked instead to earn her bread by using what she saw.
Nonetheless it worried him as, now weighing thirty stones,
He knew that this reduced the chance he'd live to make old bones.

A full twelve months of tight control and down to twelve stone, five,
Feeling like a newborn babe and glad to be alive,
Whilst walking down the High Street he aspied old Gypsy Lee,
And thinking how she got it wrong so filled his mind with glee
As he ran across to greet her-ignoring all the shouts-
A pizza van fulfilled fate's plan by crushing out his doubts.

YE TRUE EVENT FROM YE TIME OF GOOD QUEEN BESS

T'was in the Chapel-Royal, at a time of silent prayer,
That a terrible explosion befouled the hallowed air.
Though the sound was truly awful, the smell was even worse,
And far too hard to capture in just fourteen lines of verse.
Unlike many of her courtiers, who quickly ran away,
Their sovereign liege, Elizabeth, decided she must stay.
Though she'd hoped to beard the rogue
who'd wrought the frightful deed,
She soon found her will frustrated, for mounted on his steed,
An ashen Earl of Oxford, fleeing westward to his wife,
Had favoured isolation to the taking of his life.
When seven dreary years had passed he felt entirely sure
That the grievous crime which caused his shame
was thought about no more.
But the Queen, when she greeted him, loosed off a wicked dart:
"Why, my Lord of Oxford! And I had quite forgot the fart".

THE NATIVE ENGLISH PLUM

I sometimes eat a seedless grape
And rather like their juice-taut shape.
But though expected by the sick
With me, they don't entirely click.

I have a grapefruit every day,
But this seems work much more than play.
For whilst they help contain my waist,
I'm not too partial to their taste.

Of summer fruits which come in June
I eat too much, on cream-decked spoon.
So, as befits an annual fad,
When they run out, I'm almost glad.

If we now turn to peach and pear,
They're fruits of which I've had my share.
One shortcoming makes me chary,
Their flavours do so widely vary.

For just one fruit I'll beat the drum
And that's our native English plum.
Their brilliant hues, their heav'nly taste,
They stand as jewels to tawdry paste.

Czar, Pershore, Blaison Red, Gage, Belle -
Mere listing makes my taste buds swell -
Then comes, O Mundi Gloria,
Queen - Empress, the great Victoria.

NATURAL REJECTION

He: It's not that we'd be doing wrong,
It's just our genes are far too strong.
That young man whose arm you grace
Has much too much of life to face.
Perhaps he'll prove a rising star,
But there again, he mayn't go far.
Deep down you know your choice of mate
Cannot be left to whims or fate.
Your clever brain, on seeing me,
Could spot at once, subconsciously,
That as a man whose made the grade,
I'd see your favours were repaid….
With such outstanding DNA
That all our young would join the fray
Equipped to reach the highest strata
Once polished at my alma mater.
I see you blanche when pressed so hard.
Fear not, your youth would not be marred.
By virtue of that famous pill
Our genes succumb to human will.

She: I blanch because I feel so sick
You'd try on me so stale a trick.
You ought to know, you sad old fool,
I did the Darwin stuff at school.
Yes, Alpha Males can do the biz.,
But, unlike you, they've still got fizz.
Your best is in the past it seems,
So will we couple? – In your dreams!

CONSUMED WITH PLEASURE

I loves me pipe of baccy; I loves me jug of beer,
And if you buys me whisky, I'll drink it don't you fear.
I like to go to Blackpool as well as Spain or France,
And I would love to see America, just given half a chance.
I loves talking to my life-long pals at the Duck & Goose
And chatting with the ladies - if they're not too loose.
I likes chomping on my beef-steak, as well as apple pie,
And each year when the cherries come, my joy is such, I cry.
But what I love above the rest, and that includes a bet,
Is provin' to me missus that there's life in the old dog yet!

DECEMBER SONG

My heart leaps when I see her, but I really can't think why,
In the six months I've known her, I've done little else but cry.
I have never had a woman, and now I feel a fool,
The one I've set my cap at, loves me not at all.

I tried the usual blandishments like chocolates and drink,
And once I sought to kiss her when I trapped her by the sink.
As the look she then gave me would have felled a full-grown ox,
I quickly switched to useful gifts like mittens, scarves and socks.

With kindnesses and compliments I was wonderfully free,
And then I blew my pension on some silken lingerie.
Having no experience, I've just had to work by book;
Yet despite my best endeavours, I've been told to sling my hook.

Now I sit in darkness having neither love nor food,
And all because this haughty Miss thought me rather rude
When, crushed by her rejection, I said, knowing how she feels,
I'd rather that she stayed away and stuffed her meals on wheels.

LADIES WHO GLOW

His passion was the glow-worm, those little female specks
Who beam out like a lighthouse to snare the other sex;
And as a man of ample means, he had the space and time
To give to these the magic years we humans call our prime.

But he chanced upon a widow and she began to hatch
A scheme to land her daughter a very wealthy match.
Acting out a cunning plan; at last she caught his eye!
So he who'd never messed with girls thought it time to try.

Shyly, he spoke to mother first, before he pressed his suit,
And hoping to enchant him, she informed the lovelorn coot
Her daughter's very thoughts of him caused the kind of state
That overtakes the glow-worm who spots the perfect mate.

But this, instead of charming him, caused the simple soul
To drop daughter just as quickly as he would a red-hot coal.
Although he loved his beetles, he couldn't face the sight
Afforded by a woman whose bottom glowed at night.

AN OLD MAN REGRETS

Each time I see some lovely locks
I yearn to lie without my socks,
My shirt, my tie, my woolly vest,
My underpants and all the rest
On silken sheet, with her, in bed
My forearm holding up my head,
As I survey a scene so fair,
My lungs both burn for want of air.

But as I'm old, my hair all grey,
Past my prime, I've had my day,
Chasing girls is plainly loco,
So I'll just sit and sip my cocoa!

THE LEOPARD'S SPOTS

He'd always been a libertine, a man of catholic taste;
He left his lovers feeling used and very far from chaste.
All thought that this would always be, his nature being so
That once he'd had his wicked way, he simply had to go.

But now he'd met a special girl and, transfixed by darts of love,
All thoughts of others were expunged by Kay, his turtle dove.
She ruled his heart, she ruled his mind and kept him on the straight,
And everywhere her face he saw, in mirror, pool or plate.

Reflecting how this twist of fate had so transformed his life,
He sought once more to show his love to she who'd be his wife.
Turning round to catch her eye, his glance somehow missed her,
For it was caught, just a shade too long, by her charming little sister.

A DAIRY TALE

There's some within my family believe a tale so dark
It is perhaps the grimmest since the floating of the Ark.
They'll not hear of Mayerling, or that little spat at Troy,
Instead, they talk of Auntie Flo and poor old Uncle Roy.

Now Aunt Flo was wed a virgin, as pure as driven snow,
And though within a year, Roy, a soldiering had to go,
Whilst he was fighting Rommel in places like Tobruk,
She stood firm in Blighty, telling Yanks to sling their hook.

It was under the wings of Victory that things began to sour.
In a tired and grey old England, short of food and power,
To eke out a harsh existence they decided to let a room,
And accepted as a lodger, a dairyman called Croome.

To Royston it seemed like heaven, a veritable dream;
A steady weekly rental, plus butter, milk and cream.
Though seemingly a kindly man, Croome soon proved a fraud.
He had an appetite for flesh, the flesh of Auntie Maude.

Obsessed by all that food, Roy saw not his wife suborned,
But as he hit eighteen stone, as a cuckold, he was horned.
Some say that when, at last, he learned his wife a tart,
His very quick departure; 'twas death by broken heart.

But I'm a man of science; I don't buy old stuff like that;
What really caused old Royston's death was too much bloody fat!

A CHRISTMAS FAREWELL

When I compare thee to a Christmas Day,
Thou seem'st more fractious than a child up late.
And this affair at which we listless play,
A tired old turkey well past its sell-by date.

Now if, by chance, I engage your eyes,
Which once would trigger deep desire,
I see instead two stale mince pies
Which, unwanted, wither by the fire.

Once the gift for which I had lifelong yearned,
Once an angel for whom my heart long sang;
Now contempt is what you've richly earned,
A tawdry little cracker, without bang.

In short, though saying this seems cruel and rough,
Frankly, my plum, I think you somewhat duff.

PART TWO

The Serious Stuff

From the Romantic through the Reflective to the Tragic.

WILL YOU STILL LOVE ME?

Your restless turning as you weep
Draws me from the depths of sleep;
And now awake, I can feel
For you, some threat is all too real.

You sob that love so fawns on youth
We must confront the bitter truth,
As ageing slowly saps the heart,
We'll share a home, but dwell apart.

I answer that this might be true
Were I just me and you just you;
But all these years together spent
Mean what's exchanged is more than lent.

Lives lived as one a fusion form
Which, if not starved or cruelly torn,
Can yield up bonds whose strength belies
The line down which Time's arrow flies.

So sleep, my darling, in my arms
Assured that I will find your charms
As lovely in the morning light
As when the sun gave way to night.

A PREVIOUS LIFE

Never having been there,
My Italy is made up of bits and pieces.
Cyclists which owe much to Breton onion sellers
And donkey carts which draw on felt mementos
From Spain. The landscape alone seems right –
This because it's a stretch of the A44 near Pershore
Which, to me, somehow looks Italian.

No doubt, a visit would improve the detail,
But it would not alter the essentials.
The facts are clear. My future wife, then 13,
Was travelling by car in Italy with her family.
All day the road was bordered by a grass verge,
On to which her father drove in the late evening.
Unfortunately, it wasn't there. Instead,
The leading wheel entered a void.
As the angle of approach was shallow,
Breaking held the lost wheel close to the edge.
The car came to a halt, poised over a 200-foot drop.
A carefully co-ordinated exit turned near disaster
Into an adventure.

Learning of it a decade later, it seemed to me strange
That, as I struggled one-sidedly with 'O' levels,
In Italy, the better part of my life hung in the balance.

THOUGHT TO BE FROM A FAIR LADY

She says that I outmatch a summer's day,
My warmness doth engender passion's heat.
What started with the easy face of play,
Now has my lover prostrate at my feet.

And I at hers; this bond to me is all,
What lies outside are shadows without force.
My blood, long tranquil, when quickened by her call,
Soon has love's heralds hastening through its course.

And yet this love will wither by degree.
We cannot grant the crowning touch it lacks.
No mirror shows what her mind's eye can see,
And, doubtless, my hopes far outstrip the facts.

These fantasies, cruelly, our limit's set:
Blind, sterile, couplings on the Internet.

BE NOT PASSION'S SLAVE

Workers in some ivory towers
Strove to pass the idle hours,
Not by transmuting lead to gold,
But seeking out a rule which told
When men of high or low estate
Can prudently desert their mate.
They found that he who hates his wife
Should very quickly quit her life;
But if before temptation comes
A man and wife are best of chums -
Perhaps not burned in passion's heat
But finding solace fit and mete -
He should cast off his paramour
And stay within the Church's law.
This is a rule which some defy,
But they soon see, as passions die,
Lover becoming much like the wife
And that they've made a mess of life.
Too late they seek to mend their ways,
A bond once broken, broken stays.
So consider not a second bride;
As Eisenhower's a better guide.
When Ike was just about to roam,
He took a shower and went back home.

THE EVOLUTION OF LOVE

or

Knowing More Than's Good for You.

The modern heirs of Darwin, who never stop for play,
Have now thought up a new idea which blows my mind away.
It concerns the early humans who shared parental cares
By traipsing round the open veldt in tightly bonded pairs.

When it came to picking partners, it was clear to all the rest,
It's a basic law of nature that "the better gets the best".
No matter how they yearned for her, the fairest naked ape,
If she got a better offer, that's the one she'd take.

In terms of evolution this could cause a lot of grief
'Cos pairings made with second best are very often brief.
Before the day of equal pay this proved much more than sad
As a single mother's prospects were almost always bad.

Then, up there popped a little gene, a very clever chap,
Who specified the blue-print for that oh so tender trap.
We still peruse the talent with a very steely eye,
And still we note, regretfully, that some are ranked too high.

But once we've made our choice, we now forget all those above
By letting rip the hormones that will make us fall in love.
So though its many mysteries are very widely sung,
Love is just a clever trick which helps us raise our young.

But this then brings up the question: even if it is true,
Is this the kind of finding that you want revealed to you?
Perhaps we should tell those guys that, if they are very smart,
They'll poke and pry some other place and leave alone the heart.

A UNISEX JOHN DONNE FOR THE TWENTY-FIRST CENTURY

Friends, we're not islands, each with sep'rate goal,
We're like continents, one transcendent whole.
Though vast if these lose land, a price is paid,
Cliff, croft or clod, the whole is lesser made.
As when cruel seas reduce a landmass thus,
Another's passing must diminish us.
Involved, participants in every case,
We are as one with all the human race.
So ask not who's mourned, knowing this is true:
Whoever's died, the bell rings out for you.

BE KIND TO YOURSELF

'O wad some Pow'r the giftie gie us
To see oursels as others see us'
'To A Louse' Robert Burns

I think old Rabbie got it wrong,
Our world would not last very long
If we could see with steely eye
The self that's seen by passers-by.

The human brain's perhaps the best
But in one way it fails the test.
In planning all our clever acts
We need a mind which faces facts.

Yet one such fact we deeply fear:
There ain't much point in being here.
As billions of us come and go,
From whence and whither we don't know,

Our egos need stout walls and roof
To shield them from this dreadful truth.
So, whilst outwardly there's no sign,
Inside ourselves we build a shrine.

There, raised upon a noble plinth,
Which stands within a labyrinth,
There dwells the sacred sense of self
So crucial to our mental health.

These gods, who hold us all in thrall,
Demand delusions shared by all,
Which serve to fool the human race
That everyone's a special case.

So, when your mind to ego turns
Forget about old Rabbie Burns.
As of yourself you take a view,
Wear spectacles of rose red hue.

SHIVA

I've learned that though we picture him, as the cloud unfurls,
   Thinking "Now I am become Shiva, destroyer of worlds",
In fact, Oppenheimer cried "It works!" Strange he whose blast
Reshaped the world should feel the need to polish up his past.

THE SHAMEFACED WARRIOR

I had so meant to say that you were right
When digging deeper proved that I was wrong.
Before hateful pride sealed my lips up tight
I had so meant to say that you were right.
And still, so strong the primal urge to fight,
I can't admit, as would the truly strong,
I had so meant to say that you were right.
When digging deeper proved that I was wrong.

SHADOWS

I fear the shades in ancient glades when walking in the wood,
And dread the ghost, when by the post, where the gallows stood.
I fear the owl that eerie fowl which flies without a sound
Though a fool, I dread the ghoul that dwells below the ground.
But lend an ear to that great fear I've kept until the last;
For I turn blue when seared right through with shadows from
my past.

THE DAYS THOU GAVE US

To new visitors it seems commonplace
In its happiness. My love's boyish face,
Poised on the edge of maturity. Part
Prefect, part master of the bush. They start
To weave their own fantasies of life-long
Bliss. The second snap shows September's song.
Though older, a cooler, northern sun above,
End of empire didn't mean the end of love.

But they do not see the missing twenty years.
The first-time round, so full of hopes and fears,
Most men seemed faithless brutes, ill-formed and crude.
The wedded state: forced sex and servitude.
First seeming different, then just like the rest,
My church had standards; and he'd failed the test.
With foolish haste, each took another mate,
And found not love, but the potency of hate.

The match re-made, we hoped for thirty years.
We got just ten. Beyond grief, beyond tears,
I asked my Lord one thing: Christ, Oh Christ,
Why persecutest thou me twice?

DEPENDING WHICH QUARTER

The human mind, a fickle thing,
Self-serving, does so quickly swing,
That when a weathervane I see
It speaks to me of constancy.

NEW MILLENNIUM

Quartered high above the Dart, we watched
As the Earth's movement wound in the new millennium.
Already famous, city vied with city for an extra fifteen minutes.
Fireworks - their chosen means of marking time -
weighed in tons, lasting fractions of an hour,
Left nothing for the morrow but charred husks.

At dawn, as if on cue, the coming of sea mist
Coincided with the first rays of the sun.
With the insolence of an invading army sure of its own power,
It filled the valley to such depth that the view was entirely lost.
After six hours, its point seemingly having been made,
It broke up and departed in good order.

They say that it is commonly a policy of Empires
To respond moderately to the first infraction,
But react with the utmost savagery to any subsequent rebellion.
Pandemics, super-volcanoes, global warming, asteroid strikes...
Perhaps what we need to fear most in the new millennium
Is Nature's second coming.

THE REASON WHY?

*On seeing a pornographer cite freedom of
expression to justify his right to publish*

With mournful face, he strikes a pose
Of studied care, because he knows
To win he must persuade the court:
When freedom was so dearly bought,
The honoured dead their bargain made
That he, unhindered, might ply his trade.

Captain Fegen saw duty clear,
Out-gunned, out-ranged he faced the *Scheer*.
Near forty charges could be lost,
So buying time at any cost
Meant steaming north to fiery hell
Whilst they turned south to run pell-mell.

As the *Jervis Bay* met its fate,
As massive shells smashed men and plate,
Who then thought that courage so raw
Would serve to tell a court of law
That men obsessed with thoughts of cash
Should make a pile from printing trash?

A PYRRHIC VICTORY

Pyrrhus, astride his war-horse, was about to quit his home
To lead his much-loved army against the power of Rome.
As the final stores were loaded, his counsellor held the rein
And very gently asked him why he chose to march again.
The king, a genial fellow, replied with easy grace
And told his loyal servant that it stared him in the face.

The Romans were then the masters of Italy and Greece
So if he could destroy them, or make them sue for peace,
He'd start to build an empire such as made his forebear "Great",
First by invading Sicily, then, were such to be his fate,
Seizing all North Africa and thus having clearly shown
He'd Alexander's qualities, he'd straight way claim his throne.

The king replied quickly when asked, having done these things,
Just what would be the pleasures that such a victory brings?
"Though King, I am a mortal, I crave women, wine and song".
"Then Sire, said Cineas "tell me, why should you wait so long?
Just send your horses to the stable, your soldiers to the plough
Step back inside your palace and enjoy those pleasures now!".

The king, seeing he was ambushed, playfully smote his friend,
Then, taking up his horse's rein, rode off to meet that end
Which makes us all remember him for victories of such cost,
No matter what he tried to do, the war itself was lost.

Yet, as now it clearly seems to us his driving force was fame,
It is some kind of victory, a word enshrines his name.

CARELESS TALK

With joy we sang the old songs that summon up the past.
Even Nodding Molly seemed to come alive at last.
And led by Gracie Jenkins, we sang with heart and soul,
She seemed so kind and natural, not acting out a role.

The session was so special because it turned back time,
In muscle, mind and manner we seemed more like our prime.
So when our carers looked at us, surely they could see
More than leaky bags of bones always wanting tea.

Then I overheard Gracie Jenkins telling all the staff
Why she thought the sing-songs were more than just a laugh.
"They work a kind of magic that draws on strength now lost;
They perk up all the oldies and cut the nursing cost".

So ev'n when we're winning, we're dancing on their strings.
Not people with a history; but obsolescent things.
So shift up little Molly, I'll sing no more my song,
As they beat out the music, I'll just nod along.

A FARMYARD OZYMANDIAS

It's now cast up midst farmyard things,
But once it bore the weight of kings.
It carried coal, it carried crooks,
It carried schoolboys, nose in books.

It carried troops, withstood the bombs -
And all those Aussies mocking Poms -
Supported priests, upheld the Law,
And bore the goods from Bangalore.

It held the gangster with scarred fists.
It helped the lovers to their trysts;
Sustained the living, bore the dead,
And two expresses, head to head.

It held the traveller to the coast;
And all the stewards making toast.
It carried cars, it carried mail
And hordes of shoppers to the sale.

It bore the sun, it bore the rain,
It bore the dreadful diesel train.
But then 'cos man's a thankless beast,
The use of timber slowly ceased.

This one was scrapped for concrete beam,
Then sold for logs to Farmer Green,
Sent by truck to rural Surrey,
And used, instead, containing slurry.

To me, this sleeper quietly says:
No matter how we spend our days,
When done, our fates the funeral pyre,
Or slow decay within the mire.

THE VICAR'S WIFE

Perhaps she thinks that God is dead,
And her old man's off his head.
Now scorning prayer, she's come to think
That solace lies in men and drink.
But whilst in strangers' beds she lies,
One nagging thought her peace denies:
Cash she spends on booze and lovers
Depends upon the faith of others.

IN A COUNTRY CHURCHYARD

Christopher Wren's Epitaph in St Paul's:
"If you seek my monument look around you."

That modern grave is decked in green
As on it nought but weeds are seen.
Soon they'll lie there, drear and rotten,
Mocking "Gone but not forgotten".

Here, built to face the old church door,
There stands the vault of one who saw
That if he chose this focal spot,
His life would never be forgot.
Alas, though we now muse on cost,
All thoughts of him are long since lost.

These two tombs our futures presage,
Passing on the sombre message:
When we depart this earthly sphere,
Of most all thoughts soon disappear.

This serves to show Wren's son was right.
A graves a thought provoking sight,
But hopes that folks remember you
Rest not on graves but what you do.

THE SEVEN-YEAR ITCH

This little dog, whose ears I tease,
In its short life will always please;
And seeing this my lover sighs
Whilst half-formed tears enmist her eyes.
She does not speak, she makes no scene,
But I know well what those signs mean.

For once 'twas she who filled my life
With love transcending child and wife.
Then, having waxed, this could but wain,
And now will never rise again.

Such thoughts conceive a strange conceit
Which though most bleak, is sadly mete:
Is love bound, when sent from Heaven,
By the canine rule of seven.

THE VIEW FROM THE TOP

Overheard in a Dunstable junkshop on a wet Saturday afternoon.
"For nearly forty years we have laboured -or perhaps I
should say, not laboured -under the misapprehension
the world owes us a living. Unfortunately.…."

The old radio, patinated in dust,
Struggles against the voices of two men
Discussing a recent injury
To the hand of the younger. Unemployed
Nine months, within three days of starting
A new job, an accident with sheet steel
Had left a finger badly crushed. The choice
Lay between months of slow restoration
Or amputation; between loss of job
Or loss of finger. He had chosen the latter,
Jobs being scarcer than fingers.

The radio cuts back in: "We will never
Recover our pre-eminence until
We recover our willingness to work".

I step out into the rain.

WINTER OF DISCONTENT

As a late wasp labours through its final round,
I hear above the slow, still threatening sound,
Two well-dressed ladies in their middle years
Tell, feelingly, how fathers' mourning tears
Have dried to arid inactivity.

They give similar accounts: men whose lives
Shrank to weary impotence once their wives
Had died. Depressed, less keen on soap and water,
Grudging, sad, their needs demand each daughter
Draw deep on love and duty.

Lord, I pray thee, just like my brother Wasp,
Let me not withstand late autumn's frost.

HARDY'S PERENNIALS

In 1915, Thomas Hardy wrote In Time of 'The Breaking of Nations', a poem in which he expressed a firm conviction that the rural way of life he so loved, with its intimate dependence on the land he immortalised as "Wessex", would long outlive the annals of war and the dynasties responsible for them.

Tom, knowing what you hoped would be,
I think it better you can't see
The field you thought we'd still harrow,
Is cleared of hawk and cleansed of sparrow.
And this because, where once worked plough,
They've planted rows of houses now.

The Squire's gone, the Vicar too,
All local bonds are severed through.
The agri-biz which owns the lot
Is working on a fiendish plot
Extracting genes from spaniel tears
And growing wheat with great big ears.

They've felled the hedge, filled the ditch
And repossessed the football pitch.
You'd know the village, neat and trim,
But wouldn't guess who lives therein.
The locals all their birthrights sold
To townies with their bags of gold.

The school is closed, the shop is shut;
They've boarded up the old scout hut.
New owners simply come to rest
And think a child's a noisy pest.
Where hundreds heard the rising lark
There's ten machines and one bored clerk.

The rural poor have gone to dwell
In bleak estates they hate like hell.
They're fearful when their infants play,
Their abler children move away,
And all the while their less bright sons
Are smoking pot and thinking guns.

And, Thomas, there is one thing more,
We humans still have lots of War.

THE WAY AHEAD

Twenty years older, he gives advice unsought.
Climbing before me at the measured pace,
He turns slowly, and seeming lost in thought,
Surveys what he has passed and I must face.

Then, looking down, he slowly points the way.
Strength lost as muscles turn to fat,
Serious endeavour fades away to play.
Feed the family yields to "feed the cat".

Well-worn, the body fails by small degrees.
Whilst fitful sleep usurps the youthful log,
Gravity and girth conspire against the knees.
Pointlessly, worry stirs the old black dog.

Unvarnished truth, or the sourness of age?
Timely advice, or embittered, time-worn sage?

REVERSAL OF FORTUNE

*'A free translation of a parable said to have
been current in the Ancient World'*

A poor man, oppressed by life, seeking to hang himself,
Climbs to fix the noose. Finding gold hid high upon a shelf,
He goes on his way rejoicing. Discovering it not there,
The owner takes up the rope and dies in black despair.

And thus it seems our destiny turns not on love or hate
But rather on the twists and turns of something we call fate.

THE LAST ENEMY

We are packing up the transports and moving up the line
Because poor old Uncle Charlie passed on at half past nine.
There's still our Auntie Vera, but once she's been overrun,
The Nineteen Twenties Infantry will be entirely done.

When we learned "all humans die" it seemed an abstract thing.
Just a message meant for others, to us it had no sting.
For most, life's opening battles were not concerned with death,
We were seeking out our fortune, not eeking out our breath.

The few early casualties were deemed a different breed;
And even if death came so close we had to pay it heed,
We rarely mused in general terms why folks must vanish thus,
Instead we parsed with selfish care each death's effect on us.

But once in the middle years, where the annual levy swells
As death's cruel attritions or its sudden shots and shells
Wreak havoc on the cohort of our older kin and friends,
We're left with no illusions as to how this warfare ends.

So when we've seen our vanguard all perish at their posts,
We must occupy the trenches now largely filled by ghosts.
And in this lies another truth that's harder still to face,
As we give up the struggle - our children take our place.

DEATH IN THE MORNING

Like much else in nature, the need for food
Explains why the fledgling rocks back and forth.
In the nest, it's the most active of the brood
That's fed the best. A chick that bobs will grow.

There's no food now; though mother's here. She lies
By the door. Half stripped of feathers, broken-
Bodied, hopelessly past flight; when she tries,
There's a horror of ineffective fluttering.

Machine sleek on canned butchery, my cat
Has done its worst. Taken outside, the mother's
Soon dispatched. The chick, less mauled, blind and fat,
Tries what it knows and bobs in mute appeal.

Two blows and it's done; certain, swift and kind.
So why's that chick still bobbing in my mind?

SECOND CONSULTATION

Of course, I loved my mother; don't we all?
She had her faults, slovenly, sometimes cruel,
But we can't help what we are. My Aunt Ruth
Called her a slut who got lucky. There's truth
In that. I guess that she snared my father
As a result of pregnancy. Rather
Sordid; but he never knew what he'd bought.
Within six months, on his last op., he caught
A hail of flack over Bremen. So I
Didn't know him. But my yearning to fly
Was inspired by what he'd been. I had
My education paid for by his dad.
Each time I came home there was a new man
With his feet under the table. I can
Still feel the dread as I walked up the path.
Filth in the kitchen and scum in the bath.
Our educations helped weaken the link.
I was private school and Cambridge. I think
She left a state school at twelve. Such a gap
Is either the cause of pride or it'll sap
The common bond. In our case the latter.
There was nothing specifically the matter;
We just lost touch.

Oh no, not the business about the cash
For the sports car. I sensed I had been rash
To mention that. I know that I began
To blub talking about it, but I ran
Out of steam. Silly nonsense with the pills
had only just happened. Don't think it fills
My life. It's not important. It's all past.
Go over the facts? Provided it's the last
Time we talk about it. It was thirty five
Years ago, for Christ's sake. Why do you strive

To make something out of nothing? I bailed
out over jungle when my engine failed.
It took me three weeks to walk back to base.
Reported missing, believed killed; had to face
The fact that my mother now thought me dead.
Telegrams unanswer'd; strange thoughts in my head,
I was given some leave. As I arrive
Back home, I can see, on my mother's drive,
A new car. Mother's off on the wrong foot.
Truculent not sorry; I'm asked to put
Myself in her place. Son's dead, she and Stan
Need a car. They looted my Morgan
Fund the day they heard. Yet she took the line,
If fault there was, the fault was somehow mine.
So after that, we never met again.
I soon forgot; there was no lasting pain.

Why was it I never married? I just
Didn't find a girl I could really trust.
Even you can't blame my mother for that.

DOING UNTO OTHERS...

Roger Fouts, speaking with tight-reined passion,
Told us that at least sixteen years had passed
Between their having parted, his task finished,
And the occasion on which they'd met last.

For the chimpanzee the language learning
Project gave way to medical research,
Where holding disease at bay means earning
A lifetime's solitary confinement.

When given a chance of visiting him,
The anthropomorphic lie made Fouts sure
That recognition was impossible.
An ape's long-term recall is thought too poor.

But once forced into focus, Booee's eyes
Spoke immediately. Then, like a man
Almost frozen, who, in extremis, tries
To reach new-seen light, he began to move.

Desperate to restart once shared routines,
His brain drove reluctant bone and sinew.
Fouts saw through misting eyes; then, unable
To bear more, with quick clumsiness, withdrew.

Now his memory holds a final scene.
A chimp, not screaming in frustrated rage,
But sinking down, as if the whole world's been
Put back on his shoulders, crushing out hope.

Those who thus serve his kind are not evil;
Just poor, sorry fools, wrong in what they do.
He's beyond justice, but others are not;
Fouts spoke, I wrote, what should be asked of you?

JOHN KIPLING'S VILLANELLE

'My son was killed while laughing at some jest. I would I knew
What it was, and it might serve me in a time when jests are few'.
Rudyard Kipling

Sometimes it's better to let the child lead;
To stand back, leaving them to chose their stance.
This I have learned partly because I love to read.

Take how Kipling, to meet his country's need,
Pulled strings to give his son a fighting chance;
He should have left the boy to take the lead.

John, myopic, only just from the schoolroom freed,
Was all too soon 'midst mud and blood in France.
All this I know because I love to read.

They said he died joking, gave fear no heed.
In fact, he wept, face smashed in some advance,
Thinking, no doubt, how father took the lead.

I have a son, like his, a last of breed;
But my task is to shield him from mischance.
This I know, partly, because I love to read.

If war comes, I'll not follow Kipling's creed.
To fight or not, my son shall choose his stance.
Sometimes it's best that the child takes the lead;
This I know not just because I love to read.

MOTHER'S BOY

Not like our usual session on the links.
Nasty business, quite shook me up. Doc thinks
It was always on the cards; but that's news to me.
Of course, recently our talk's been less free,
But I was certain, after twenty years,
I knew what made her tick. Some tears
Perhaps, never guessed she'd take her own life.
Must say, it's a bad time to lose a wife.
No doubt you know I'm up for mayor next year;
but a whiff of scandal and I'm done for. Mere
Flirtation sunk old Brown. To stay afloat
I need your help. Why? My wife's left a note.
In it she spills the beans. Before she died
We'd had a row. She said that I had lied
And cheated throughout all our married life;
That she was leaving and, having so good
A case against me, a court of law would
Grant her custody of our boy. Hard pressed,
I played my ace. Because we'd not been blessed
With natural issue, our son's adopted.
She thought we had taken under our wing
The child, born without benefit of ring,
"Father Unknown" to our au pair. Only
The mother knew the boy was mine. Lonely,
Shamed by her own barrenness, my wife pressed
The girl to give up the child. Though distressed
At first, she soon saw sense when I made clear
That this was best for all concerned. The fear
And hate in my wife's eyes when told of this
Shook me. But I made sure she did not miss
The fact my claim on the boy was greater.
I told her "Act in haste, rue it later",
And, a meeting to attend, I left her
To reflect. Instead, to cause the biggest stir
Possible, she threw herself under a train.

Police found the note and I've wracked my brain
To think of some way to play it down.
Then I remembered – please don't start to frown –
You're in the coroner's lodge. There's no need
To bend the rules. It's up to him. Just plead
On my behalf that the note be kept out
Of open court. Do it, and don't ever doubt
I'll make it worth your while. A new sea wall
Is on the cards; I'm sure a well-judged call
For a local firm to get the job should
Tip the scales your way. It's something I would
Do once my little problem's disappeared.
With council jobs the trick's in how they're steered.
But please don't think I'm always on the make.
"We pass this way but once" 's the line I take.
Some see their neighbours as foes not brothers;
But my creed's: "Help ease the life of others".

THE BEARMAN

The youngest child, despite the privations
Of war, was bright and confident. Nations
Might founder, but, for the child, birth order
Counts much more than distant carnage. Broader
Shoulders carried a greater load. Mother -
Her first-born in the Air Force, his brother,
The Navy - lived in constant, drum-taut fear
Of the postboys knock.

The child's disposition made the nightmare
The more surprising. Seeming free of care,
She'd been put to bed. The scream made them freeze.
"Stop the bearman, stop the bearman, please, please,
Stop the bearman". Once with her, they worked
To quell the dread, showing that no bear lurked
Within her room. With them to protect her,
She would always be safe and secure.

The telegram came the next day. Bear-stout,
To protect against cold and flak; without
Comfort, as his sister started crying,
The eldest boy had just made his dying,
Hopeless, pleas for Mother.
For the child, there were no more nightmares.

ANOTHER TIME

We Flanders dead in silence curse
The fools who think a poet's verse
Can give them all the reasons why
We came to France to fight and die.
Because we fought as we could see
Our freedoms hung on victory,
We're pained to learn that we're each drawn
A self-deluding, ill-led pawn.

Now poets are a special kind
Whose words can shape the human mind;
But one small point is sometimes missed,
For want of grit, they're often grist.
We steady men who held the line,
Clear in head and firm in spine,
Did not march out as Empire's sons
And nor because we loathed the Huns.

It's just we knew Germanic will
Would never, never have its fill.
Once they'd consumed the Russian horde,
They'd toast the Frenchman on his sword.
Next, and at a time that they judged mete,
They'd build the ships to match our fleet.
Then, all of Europe 'neath their thumbs,
They'd scour the world in search of plums.

Men facing tigers know this rule:
Attack by turn, he'll have you all.
So, as fight we must, we chose a day
With other Powers still in play.
To our cold eyes your world is rotten
As in it this stark rule's forgotten:
A course though deadly, hard and long
By these alone is not made wrong.

You moderns think you should be spared
The kinds of suffering we all shared;
Then be prepared, our young kin-folk,
To bend your necks to foreign yoke.

AND THIS WE CALL LOVE

Both young, she gave him the love he needed,
Thawed by its warmth, his stammer receded.
Just engaged, when they went to a dance,
Sensing attraction, a man seized his chance.
Becoming his mistress cost her her life.
As back to the wall, he chose children and wife.
Then – something with which he struggled to cope –
The girl had been found at the end of a rope.
As for the boy so cruelly betrayed,
His stammer returned and this time it stayed.

Others were burned - beyond the above -
But this is the force we choose to call love.

Printed in Great Britain
by Amazon